Coach Hargitt does a terrific job in his latest book of presenting 101 RPO plays that can be used at any competitive level of football. This book is a must resource for any football coach who is looking to add a game-changing element to his offense.

Slade Singleton
Offensive Coordinator
Madison High School (NC)

Coach Hargitt's new book, *101 RPO Plays*, is a great resource for coaches wanting to incorporate RPOs into their team's offense. Coach Hargitt has a great offensive mind and offers great insight for those coaches who have decided to take their offense to the next level.

Jeff Harper
Quarterbacks Coach
Loyola College Prep (LA)
Owner/Private Quarterback Coach,
Gunslinger Quarterback Academy

Coach Hargitt has been my go-to guy concerning up-tempo offenses for years. His insights, concepts, and principles are always ahead of the curve of where football is trending. *101 RPO Plays* is an instructional asset that can help every football coach.

Robert Aurilio
Offensive Coordinator
Montini Catholic High School (IL)
6-time Illinois State Champions

101 RPO Plays offers a one-stop package of state-of-the-art plays, featuring the hottest offensive topic in the game—RPOs.

Fabian Herlemann
Head Coach/Athletic Director
ASC Leipzig (Germany) HAWKS e.V.

101 RPO Plays features cutting edge information, insights, and ideas. The days of three yards and a cloud of dust are long gone. Learning and implementing the RPO plays in Coach Hargitt's compelling book will help you stress defenses both vertically and horizontally. You will also learn how to put defenders into conflict and force them to defend the entire field.

Tony Rodriguez
Offensive Coordinator
East Bay High School (FL)

101
RPO Plays

Rich Hargitt

ISBN: 978-1-60679-408-1
Library of Congress Control Number: 2017946251
Cover design: Cheery Sugabo
Book layout: Cheery Sugabo
Front cover photo: ©Del Mecum/CSM via ZUMA Wire

Coaches Choice
P.O. Box 1828
Monterey, CA 93942
www.coacheschoice.com

Dedication

This work is dedicated to my wonderful wife, Lisa, and our beautiful sons, Griffin and Graham. Thanks to my wife for all the endless support in coaching and to my sons for showing me what is really important in this life. Finally, this work is dedicated above all to God, who gives me the ability to live each day with strength and honor.

Acknowledgments

I would like to thank my beautiful wife, Lisa, and our sons, Griffin and Graham, who support me. Thanks also to my parents, who gave me the foundation to be a successful coach.

I would like to thank a wide variety of coaches who have helped me learn a great deal about the spread offense in general and the air raid version of it in particular. First, I would like to thank the father of the air raid offense, Hal Mumme, who has offered unquestionably good insight into the offense that he has helped to pioneer. I would also like to thank Matt Mumme, the offensive coordinator at Davidson College in Davidson, North Carolina; Marc Kolb, the offensive coordinator at Tusculum College in Greenville, Tennessee; Stan Zweifel and Jake Olsen of the University of Dubuque; and Dale Carlson, the head football coach at Valparaiso University in Valparaiso, Indiana. Fellow high schools coaches have helped in numerous ways to provide me with insight into various aspects of the spread offense and the air raid offense. These generous coaches include: Brent Eckley of Jackson High School (MO), Matt Beam of Burns High School (NC), Lee Sadler of Mountain Home High School (AR), John Allison of Sacred Heart Griffin High School (IL), Ken Leonard of Sacred Heart Griffin High School (IL), Derek Leonard of Rochester HS (IL), Mark Grounds of Jacksonville High School (IL), Brian Hales of Butler High School (NC), Bob Gaddis of Columbus East High School (IN), and Kevin Wright of Carmel High School (IN).

Thanks also to Jim Peterson for helping me get exposure for this offense and to the great people at Coaches Choice. Special thanks also goes out to the individuals at Glazier Clinics, Nike Clinics, and USA Football for helping grow and nurture this brand of football.

I would also like to give thanks to Coach Dave Farquharson for always being there to bounce ideas off of and traveling the country to learn more football. Secondly, thanks to Randy Niekamp for all the time on the phone and in person and for being such a source of information and support. Finally, I would like to thank DeMarcus Mullinax for his unwavering support in building the RPO system and for helping to coach it along the way.

Finally, I would like to acknowledge the athletes in Illinois, Indiana, North Carolina, and South Carolina who ran our system and worked so hard to represent their faith, family, and football program with such class.

Foreword

Adapt or Die

"Adapt or die." We hear this saying all the time. The game of football is a living organism that is constantly evolving and changing shape. The best coaches are always adapting and willing to change their ways. Rich Hargitt has made a living by constantly adapting and always being one step ahead of the curve on the offensive side of the ball.

The run-pass option (RPO) has revolutionized the game of football. At the forefront of this movement has been Rich Hargitt. Coach Hargitt's career has evolved from teaching the wing-T, to becoming an air raid expert, to now being considered one of the most innovative RPO minds in the country. This book is a deep dive inside his mind and gives the reader the feeling of being in the film room with Coach Hargitt as he draws X's and O's on the white board.

On a personal note, I consider myself extremely lucky to have Coach Hargitt as both a friend and mentor. He has been a tremendous influence on my coaching career.

I have never met a more driven individual in the coaching ranks. Coach Hargitt's relentless desire to constantly improve is unmatched. Rich's success is not an accident. He spends countless hours in the film room, attending football clinics, and studying programs of other great coaches. He is always working to improve his craft, and this is something I strive to emulate each day.

While the improvements he has helped me make as a football coach seem endless, he has impacted my life the most off the field. Coach Hargitt's ability to balance the strenuous hours of being a football coach with being a loving husband and devoted father are unmatched. Rich is a tremendous mentor and role model for our student-athletes. We need more men like him coaching this great game!

101 RPO Plays should be required reading for all coaches looking to stay at the forefront of the coaching profession. Coach Hargitt will teach you how to install, teach, and execute RPO plays with the power to make the defense wrong on every snap. There is no doubt the game of football is changing: *adapt or die*.

Garrison Carter
Head Football Coach
Washington (IA) High School

Contents

Preface

An ever-increasing trend in modern spread offenses has been to feature run-pass options (RPOs) as a basic part of the offense. The vast majority of spread offenses today not only feature some form of RPO structure, but many offenses actually make the commitment to base the majority of their offense around the idea of RPOs. There has been much discussion and a fair amount of literature on RPOs, but what has not been covered in detail is a comprehensive playbook within these RPO structures.

There has been a yearning for coaches to produce a playbook for the air raid offense and to give it teeth—in other words, to provide the reader with a real comprehensive understanding of what coaches need to be doing in order to be successful. This work dives into that conversation and gives wings to that yearning at exactly the right time. As modern offenses evolve, they are taking on the trend of being RPO-based and relying on the quarterback to get the ball into the right part of the grass on the football field at the right moment and to the right person. Therefore, the responsibility placed upon the quarterbacks has taken on an even greater degree of importance as they now do the majority of the mental heavy lifting for the offense. Hence, this work endeavors to provide a line-by-line explanation of all 11 positions on the field, but provides the most extensive explanations for the quarterback position.

It is worth pointing out how this book will consider run-pass options and how they are taught. A run-pass option is any play where the offense is given both a run play and some sort of pass or screen play simultaneously, and the quarterback makes a decision as to which play should actually be utilized. In short, the quarterback actually makes a read and a decision about which play the offense should be using in order to give it the best chance of success in that moment. For the purpose of this book, it is assumed that if the defensive end is blocked or locked, the quarterback will make 80 percent of his decision based upon the pre-snap alignment of the defense with 20 percent of his decision coming after the snap or post-snap. If the defensive end or C gap defender is unblocked, then these percentages are reversed as the quarterback will make his decision with a 20 percent pre-snap influence and an 80 percent post-snap influence. This system allows the quarterback to play fast and trust his judgment based upon what the defense presents to him for a look while also allowing him to read defenders at the snap and make the best possible decisions for the offense to be successful.

The purpose of this work is to provide a basic RPO playbook for a large, diverse, and almost continuously expanding audience of offensive as well as defensive coaches. The basic run plays of a traditional air raid offense will be broken down into their specific components and techniques, and then the reader will be provided with a sample of commonly used and successfully implemented RPOs that can give the offense the vitality to grow and adapt to the changing landscape of high school and college football. This work will provide the reader with the basis for how to teach the inside zone, outside zone, counter, power, and other varied and RPO-friendly run plays as well as teach the commonly used pass concepts that marry most effectively to a modern spread offensive system.

This work will certainly not cover every aspect of how to train offensive players or run RPOs, but it will certainly begin to provide coaches with the framework necessary to perform both functions at a very high level. The information in this work has been collected from real on-the-field experiences at the high school level over an extensive period of time. It is hoped that this work sheds new light on the importance of coaching the specific positions and how to use RPOs to improve and enable the athletes that utilize them to play at their highest level possible throughout a season.

PLAY #1: INSIDE ZONE/NOW 1

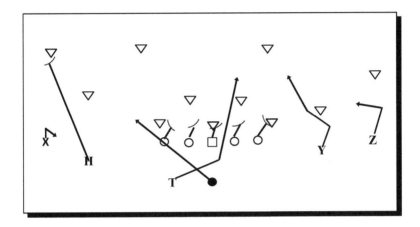

Blocking Rules:

Z: Grass

X: Screen

H: Stalk blocks #1

Y: Grass

RT: Zone

RG: Zone

C: Zone

LG: Zone

LT: Zone

TB: Open steps with near foot; crosses over and chases the inside leg of the playside tackle; cuts back if the first defender playside of the center crosses his face.

QB: Opens nearest foot to the TB; extends the ball while reading the movement of the backside C gap defender; if he closes, pulls the ball and executes an RPO.

PLAY #2: INSIDE ZONE/NOW 2

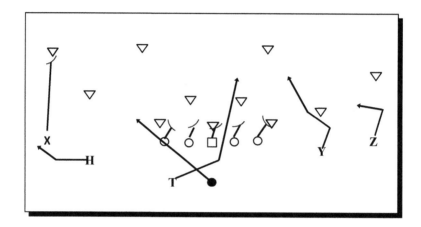

Blocking Rules:

Z: Grass

X: Stalk blocks #1

H: Screen

Y: Grass

RT: Zone

RG: Zone

C: Zone

LG: Zone

LT: Zone

TB: Open steps with near foot; crosses over and chases the outside leg of the playside tackle; does not cut back under any circumstances.

QB: Keeps feet parallel to the line of scrimmage; extends the ball while reading the movement of the backside C gap defender; if he closes, pulls the ball and executes an RPO.

PLAY #3: INSIDE ZONE/NOW 4

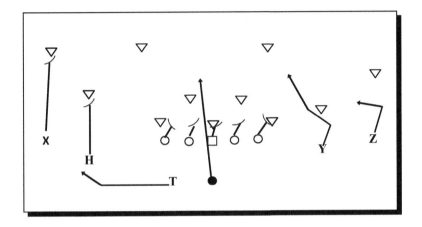

Blocking Rules:

Z: Grass

X: Stalk blocks #1

H: Stalk blocks #2

Y: Grass

RT: Zone

RG: Zone

C: Zone

LG: Zone

LT: Zone

TB: Swing screen

QB: Reads the numbers on the perimeter for the RPO. The assignment is to run the ball if the defense distorts to cover the back and to throw the ball to the back if the defense does not leave the box.

PLAY #4: INSIDE ZONE/ HITCH CONCEPT

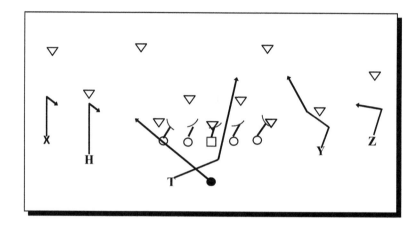

Blocking Rules:

Z: Grass

X: Hitch

H: Hitch

Y: Grass

RT: Zone

RG: Zone

C: Zone

LG: Zone

LT: Zone

TB: Zone path

QB: Pre-snap reads the grass concept side and then the hitch concept side and executes a throw if they are gifts. If the alignment of the defense prevents a pre-snap throw, meshes with the back and reads the C gap defender; if he squeezes, executes the hitch concept or runs the ball accordingly.

PLAY #5: INSIDE ZONE/ GRASS CONCEPT

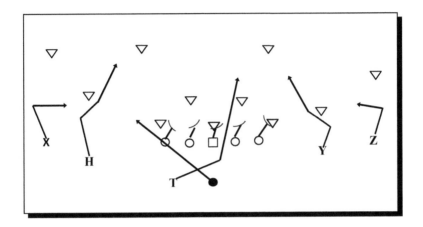

Blocking Rules:

Z: Grass

X: Grass

H: Grass

Y: Grass

RT: Zone

RG: Zone

C: Zone

LG: Zone

LT: Zone

TB: Zone path

QB: Pre-snap reads the grass concept on the zone side and then the grass concept on the backside and executes a throw if they are gifts. If the alignment of the defense prevents a pre-snap throw, meshes with the back and reads the C gap defender; if he squeezes, executes the post-snap (backside) grass concept or run the ball accordingly.

PLAY #6: INSIDE ZONE/STOP CONCEPT

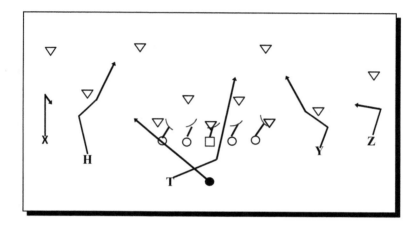

Blocking Rules:

Z: Grass

X: Stop

H: Grass

Y: Grass

RT: Zone

RG: Zone

C: Zone

LG: Zone

LT: Zone

TB: Zone path

QB: Pre-snap reads the grass concept side and then the stop concept side and executes a throw if they are gifts. If the alignment of the defense prevents a pre-snap throw, meshes with the back and reads the C gap defender; if he squeezes, executes the stop concept or runs the ball accordingly.

PLAY #7: INSIDE ZONE/ SNAG CONCEPT

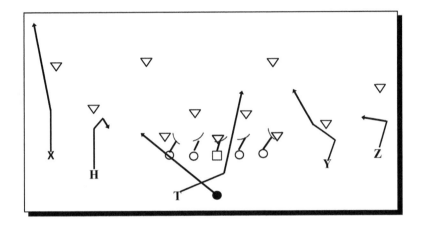

Blocking Rules:

Z: Grass

X: Fade

H: Snag

Y: Grass

RT: Zone

RG: Zone

C: Zone

LG: Zone

LT: Zone

TB: Zone path

QB: Pre-snap reads the grass concept side and then the snag concept side and executes a throw if they are gifts. If the alignment of the defense prevents a pre-snap throw, meshes with the back and reads the C gap defender; if he squeezes, executes the snag concept (post-snap) or run the ball accordingly.

PLAY #8: INSIDE ZONE/STICK CONCEPT

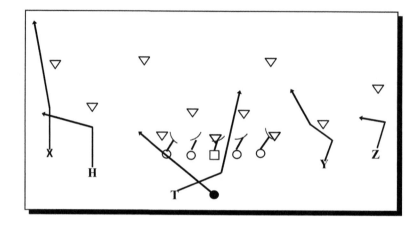

Blocking Rules:

Z: Grass

X: Fade

H: Flat

Y: Grass

RT: Zone

RG: Zone

C: Zone

LG: Zone

LT: Zone

TB: Zone path

QB: Pre-snap reads the grass concept side and then the stick concept side and executes a throw if they are gifts. If the alignment of the defense prevents a pre-snap throw, meshes with the back and reads the C gap defender, if he squeezes execute the stick concept (Post-snap) or run the ball accordingly.

PLAY #9: INSIDE ZONE/SPOT CONCEPT

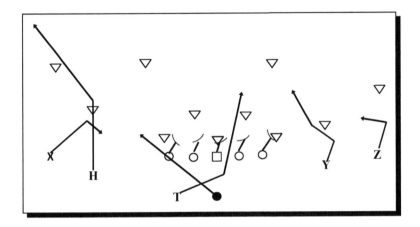

Blocking Rules:

Z: Grass

X: Spot

H: Corner

Y: Grass

RT: Zone

RG: Zone

C: Zone

LG: Zone

LT: Zone

TB: Zone path

QB: Pre-snap reads the grass concept side and then the spot concept side and executes a throw if they are gifts. If the alignment of the defense prevents a pre-snap throw, meshes with the back and reads the C gap defender; if he squeezes, executes the spot concept (post-snap) or runs the ball accordingly.

PLAY #10: 2X2 WAVE

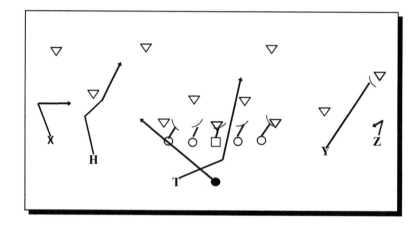

Blocking Rules:

Z: Screen

X: Grass

H: Grass

Y: Stalk blocks #1

RT: Zone

RG: Zone

C: Zone

LG: Zone

LT: Zone

TB: Zone path

QB: Pre-snap reads the right side screen and then the grass concept side and executes a throw if they are gifts. If the alignment of the defense prevents a pre-snap throw, meshes with the back and reads the C gap defender; if he squeezes, executes the grass concept (post-snap) or runs the ball accordingly. This is an example of a one-word RPO, meaning that there are three plays packaged together with one word.

PLAY #11: INSIDE ZONE/ TAPER CONCEPT

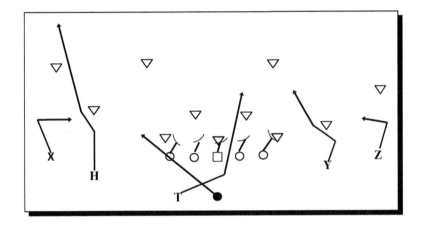

Blocking Rules:

Z: Grass

X: Speed in

H: Taper fade

Y: Grass

RT: Zone

RG: Zone

C: Zone

LG: Zone

LT: Zone

TB: Zone path

QB: Pre-snap reads the grass concept side and then the taper concept side and executes a throw if they are gifts. If the alignment of the defense prevents a pre-snap throw, meshes with the back and reads the C gap defender; if he squeezes, executes the taper concept (post-snap) or runs the ball accordingly.

PLAY #12: INSIDE ZONE/SIT CONCEPT

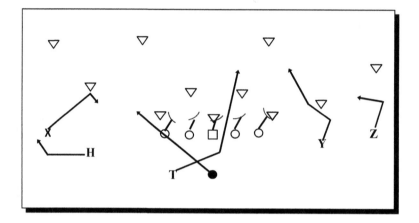

Blocking Rules:

Z: Grass

X: Sit

H: Bubble

Y: Grass

RT: Zone

RG: Zone

C: Zone

LG: Zone

LT: Zone

TB: Zone path

QB: Pre-snap reads the grass concept side and then the sit concept side and executes a throw if they are gifts. If the alignment of the defense prevents a pre-snap throw, meshes with the back and reads the C gap defender; if he squeezes, executes the sit concept (post-snap) or runs the ball accordingly.

PLAY #13: INSIDE ZONE/ SLANT OPTION CONCEPT

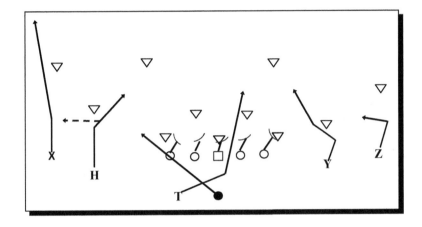

Blocking Rules:

Z: Grass

X: Fade

H: Slant/option

Y: Grass

RT: Zone

RG: Zone

C: Zone

LG: Zone

LT: Zone

TB: Zone path

QB: Pre-snap reads the grass concept side and then the slant option concept side and executes a throw if they are gifts. If the alignment of the defense prevents a pre-snap throw, meshes with the back and reads the C gap defender; if he squeezes, executes the slant option concept (post-snap) or runs the ball accordingly.

PLAY #14: INSIDE ZONE/ SLANT FLAT CONCEPT

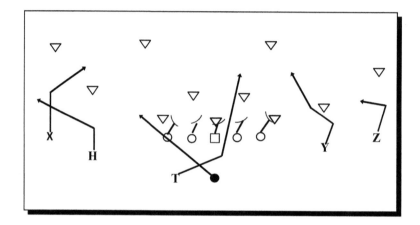

Blocking Rules:

Z: Grass

X: Slant

H: Flat

Y: Grass

RT: Zone

RG: Zone

C: Zone

LG: Zone

LT: Zone

TB: Zone path

QB: Pre-snap reads the grass concept side and then the slant flat concept side and executes a throw if they are gifts. If the alignment of the defense prevents a pre-snap throw, meshes with the back and reads the C gap defender; if he squeezes, executes the slant flat concept (post-snap) or runs the ball accordingly.

PLAY #15: INSIDE ZONE/ STUTTER CONCEPT

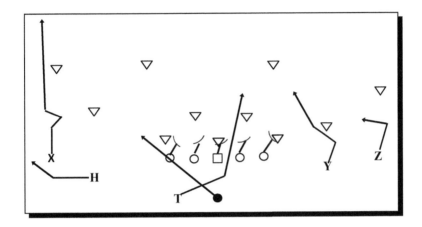

Blocking Rules:

Z: Grass

X: Stutter fade

H: Bubble

Y: Grass

RT: Zone

RG: Zone

C: Zone

LG: Zone

LT: Zone

TB: Zone path

QB: Pre-snap reads the grass concept side and then the stutter concept side and executes a throw if they are gifts. If the alignment of the defense prevents a pre-snap throw, meshes with the back and reads the C gap defender; if he squeezes, executes the stutter concept (post-snap) or runs the ball accordingly.

PLAY #16: INSIDE ZONE/BOUNCE

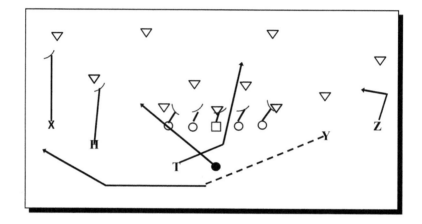

Blocking Rules:

Z: Grass

X: Stalk blocks #1

H: Stalk blocks #2

Y: Orbit motion into a swing screen

RT: Zone

RG: Zone

C: Zone

LG: Zone

LT: Zone

TB: Zone path

QB: Pre-snap reads the grass concept side and executes a throw if it is a gift. If the alignment of the defense prevents a pre-snap throw, meshes with the back and reads the C gap defender; if he squeezes, executes the swing screen (post-snap) or runs the ball accordingly.

PLAY #17: INSIDE ZONE/ BOUNCE (SPLIT)

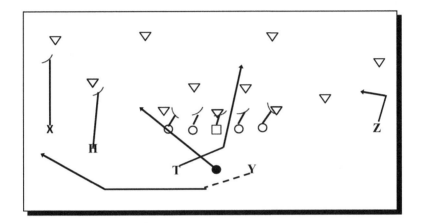

Blocking Rules:

Z: Grass

X: Stalk blocks #1

H: Stalk blocks #2

Y: Orbit motion into a swing screen

RT: Zone

RG: Zone

C: Zone

LG: Zone

LT: Zone

TB: Zone path

QB: Pre-snap reads the grass concept side and executes a throw if it is a gift. If the alignment of the defense prevents a pre-snap throw, meshes with the back and reads the C gap defender; if he squeezes, executes the swing screen (post-snap) or runs the ball accordingly.

PLAY #18: GENERAL

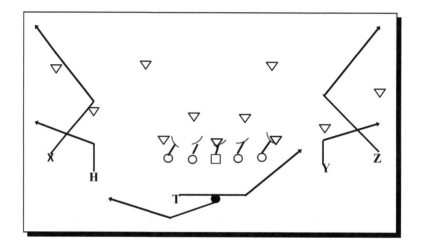

Blocking Rules:

Z: V-cut corner

X: V-cut corner

H: Flat

Y: Flat

RT: Zone and pass set

RG: Zone and pass set

C: Zone and pass set

LG: Zone and pass set

LT: Zone and pass set

TB: Outside zone path and executes a run or throw to one of the two receivers.

QB: Reads the C gap defender. If he squeezes, pulls the ball and runs the ball or executes one of the two pass routes; if the C gap defender feathers, then gives to the TB.

PLAY #19: INSIDE ZONE/NOW 1

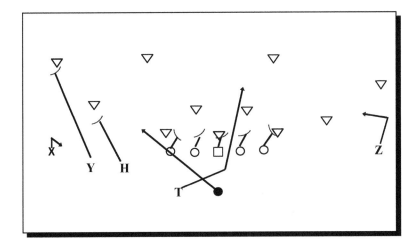

Blocking Rules:

Z: Grass

X: Screen

H: Stalk blocks #2

Y: Stalk blocks #1

RT: Zone

RG: Zone

C: Zone

LG: Zone

LT: Zone

TB: Zone path

QB: Pre-snap reads the grass concept side and then the now screen side and executes a throw if they are gifts. If the alignment of the defense prevents a pre-snap throw, meshes with the back and reads the C gap defender; if he squeezes, executes the now screen (post-snap) or runs the ball accordingly.

PLAY #20: INSIDE ZONE/NOW 2

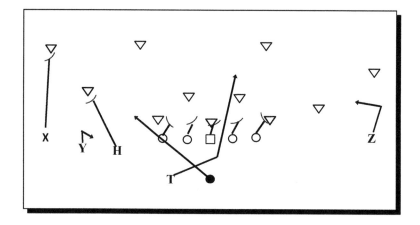

Blocking Rules:

Z: Grass

X: Stalk blocks #1

H: Stalk blocks #2

Y: Screen

RT: Zone

RG: Zone

C: Zone

LG: Zone

LT: Zone

TB: Zone path

QB: Pre-snap reads the grass concept side and then the now screen side and executes a throw if they are gifts. If the alignment of the defense prevents a pre-snap throw, meshes with the back and reads the C gap defender; if he squeezes, executes the now screen (post-snap) or runs the ball accordingly.

PLAY #21: INSIDE ZONE/NOW 3

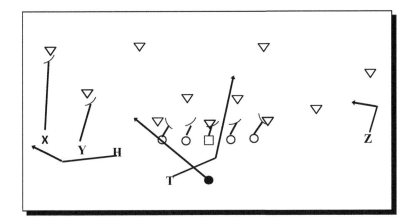

Blocking Rules:

Z: Grass

X: Stalk blocks #1

H: Screen

Y: Stalk blocks #2

RT: Zone

RG: Zone

C: Zone

LG: Zone

LT: Zone

TB: Zone path

QB: Pre-snap reads the grass concept side and then the now screen side and executes a throw if they are gifts. If the alignment of the defense prevents a pre-snap throw, meshes with the back and reads the C gap defender; if he squeezes, executes the now screen (post-snap) or runs the ball accordingly.

PLAY #22: INSIDE ZONE/NOW 4

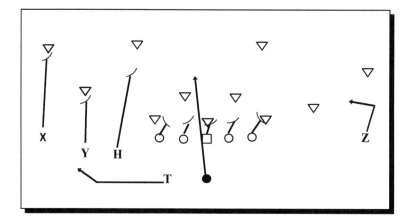

Blocking Rules:

Z: Grass

X: Stalk blocks #1

H: Stalk blocks #3

Y: Stalk blocks #2

RT: Zone

RG: Zone

C: Zone

LG: Zone

LT: Zone

TB: Swing screen

QB: Reads the numbers on the perimeter for the RPO. The assignment is to run the ball if the defense distorts to cover the back and to throw the ball to the back if the defense does not leave the box.

PLAY #23: INSIDE ZONE/ HITCH CONCEPT

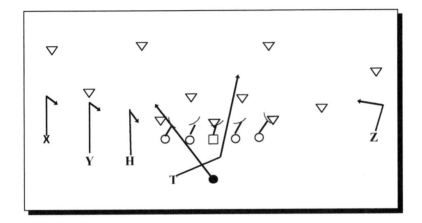

Blocking Rules:

Z: Grass

X: Hitch

H: Hitch

Y: Hitch

RT: Zone

RG: Zone

C: Zone

LG: Zone

LT: Zone

TB: Zone path

QB: Pre-snap reads the grass concept side and then the hitch concept side and executes a throw if they are gifts. If the alignment of the defense prevents a pre-snap throw, meshes with the back and reads the C gap defender; if he squeezes, executes the hitch concept (post-snap) or runs the ball accordingly.

PLAY #24: INSIDE ZONE/ GRASS CONCEPT

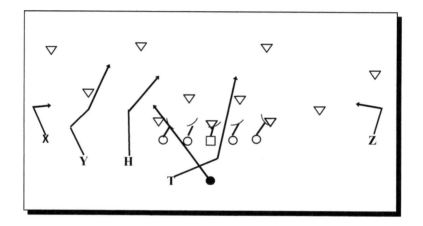

Blocking Rules:

Z: Grass

X: Grass

H: Grass

Y: Grass

RT: Zone

RG: Zone

C: Zone

LG: Zone

LT- Zone

TB: Zone path

QB: Pre-snap reads the zone run side grass concept and then the backside grass concept side and executes a throw if they are gifts. If the alignment of the defense prevents a pre-snap throw, meshes with the back and reads the C gap defender; if he squeezes, executes the backside grass concept (post-snap) or runs the ball accordingly.

PLAY #25: INSIDE ZONE/ STOP CONCEPT

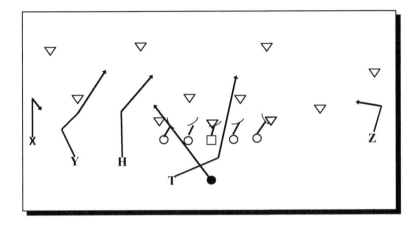

Blocking Rules:

Z: Grass

X: Stop

H: Grass

Y: Grass

RT: Zone

RG: Zone

C: Zone

LG: Zone

LT: Zone

TB: Zone path

QB: Pre-snap reads the grass concept side and then the stop concept side and executes a throw if they are gifts. If the alignment of the defense prevents a pre-snap throw, meshes with the back and reads the C gap defender; if he squeezes, executes the stop concept (post-snap) or runs the ball accordingly.

PLAY #26: INSIDE ZONE/ SNAG CONCEPT

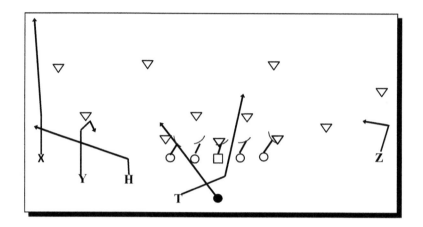

Blocking Rules:

Z: Grass

X: Fade

H: Flat

Y: Snag

RT: Zone

RG: Zone

C: Zone

LG: Zone

LT: Zone

TB: Zone path

QB: Pre-snap reads the grass concept side and then the snag concept side and executes a throw if they are gifts. If the alignment of the defense prevents a pre-snap throw, meshes with the back and reads the C gap defender; if he squeezes, executes the snag concept (post-snap) or runs the ball accordingly.

PLAY #27: INSIDE ZONE/ STICK CONCEPT

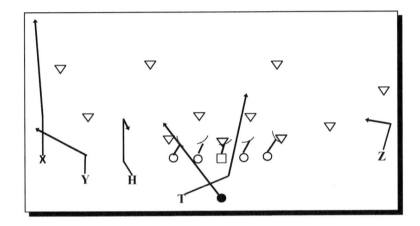

Blocking Rules:

Z: Grass

X: Fade

H: Hitch

Y: Flat

RT: Zone

RG: Zone

C: Zone

LG: Zone

LT: Zone

TB: Zone path

QB: Pre-snap reads the grass concept side and then the stick concept side and executes a throw if they are gifts. If the alignment of the defense prevents a pre-snap throw, meshes with the back and reads the C gap defender; if he squeezes, executes the stick concept (post-snap) or runs the ball accordingly.

PLAY #28: INSIDE ZONE/ SPOT CONCEPT

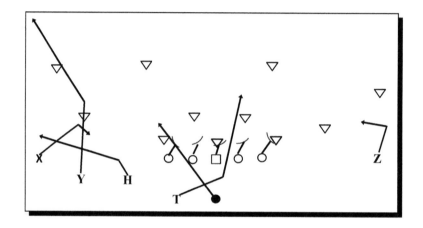

Blocking Rules:

Z: Grass

X: Spot

H: Flat

Y: Corner

RT: Zone

RG: Zone

C: Zone

LG: Zone

LT: Zone

TB: Zone path

QB: Pre-snap reads the grass concept side and then the spot concept side and executes a throw if they are gifts. If the alignment of the defense prevents a pre-snap throw, meshes with the back and read the C gap defender; if he squeezes, executes the spot concept (post-snap) or runs the ball accordingly.

PLAY #29: INSIDE ZONE/ BLAZER CONCEPT

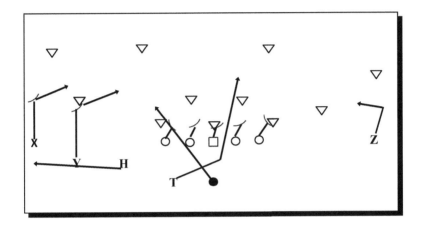

Blocking Rules:

Z: Grass

X: Stalk and slant

H: Bubble

Y: Stalk and slant

RT: Zone

RG: Zone

C: Zone

LG: Zone

LT: Zone

TB: Zone path

QB: Pre-snap reads the grass concept side and then the blazer concept side and executes a throw if they are gifts. If the alignment of the defense prevents a pre-snap throw, meshes with the back and reads the C gap defender; if he squeezes, executes the blazer concept (post-snap) or runs the ball accordingly.

PLAY #30: INSIDE ZONE/ TAPER CONCEPT

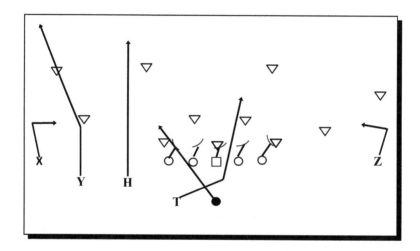

Blocking Rules:

Z: Grass

X: Speed in

H: Outside release seam

Y: Taper fade

RT: Zone

RG: Zone

C: Zone

LG: Zone

LT: Zone

TB: Zone path

QB: Pre-snap reads the grass concept side and then the taper concept side and executes a throw if they are gifts. If the alignment of the defense prevents a pre-snap throw, meshes with the back and reads the C gap defender; if he squeezes, executes the taper concept (post-snap) or runs the ball accordingly.

PLAY #31: INSIDE ZONE/SIT CONCEPT

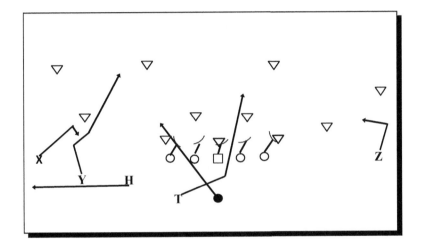

Blocking Rules:

Z: Grass

X: Sit

H: Bubble

Y: Broken arrow slant

RT: Zone

RG: Zone

C: Zone

LG: Zone

LT: Zone

TB: Zone path

QB: Pre-snap reads the grass concept side and then the sit concept side and executes a throw if they are gifts. If the alignment of the defense prevents a pre-snap throw, meshes with the back and reads the C gap defender; if he squeezes, executes the sit concept (post-snap) or runs the ball accordingly.

PLAY #32: INSIDE ZONE/ SLANT OPTION CONCEPT

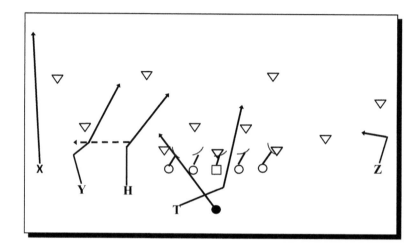

Blocking Rules:

Z: Grass

X: Fade

H: Slant option

Y: Broken arrow slant

RT: Zone

RG: Zone

C: Zone

LG: Zone

LT: Zone

TB: Zone path

QB: Pre-snap reads the grass concept side and then the slant option concept side and executes a throw if they are gifts. If the alignment of the defense prevents a pre-snap throw, meshes with the back and reads the C gap defender; if he squeezes, executes the slant option concept (post-snap) or runs the ball accordingly.

PLAY #33: INSIDE ZONE/ SLANT FLAT CONCEPT

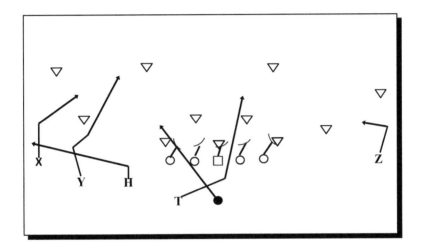

Blocking Rules:

Z: Grass

X: Slant

H: Flat

Y: Broken arrow slant

RT: Zone

RG: Zone

C: Zone

LG: Zone

LT: Zone

TB: Zone path

QB: Pre-snap reads the grass concept side and then the slant flat concept side and executes a throw if they are gifts. If the alignment of the defense prevents a pre-snap throw, meshes with the back and reads the C gap defender; if he squeezes, executes the slant flat concept (post-snap) or runs the ball accordingly.

PLAY #34: INSIDE ZONE/ STUTTER CONCEPT

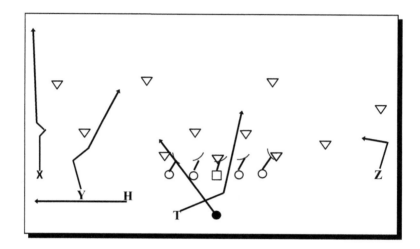

Blocking Rules:

Z: Grass

X: Stutter fade

H: Bubble

Y: Broken arrow slant

RT: Zone

RG: Zone

C: Zone

LG: Zone

LT: Zone

TB: Zone path

QB: Pre-snap reads the grass concept side and then the stutter concept side and executes a throw if they are gifts. If the alignment of the defense prevents a pre-snap throw, meshes with the back and reads the C gap defender; if he squeezes, executes the stutter concept (post-snap) or runs the ball accordingly.

PLAY #35: INSIDE ZONE/BOUNCE

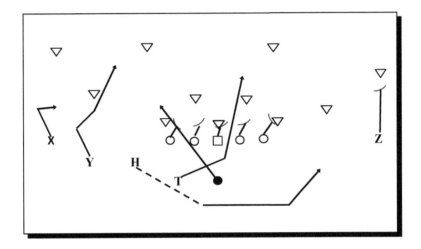

Blocking Rules:

Z: Stalk blocks #1

X: Grass

H: Goes in orbit motion and performs a swing screen

Y: Grass

RT: Zone

RG: Zone

C: Zone

LG: Zone

LT: Zone

TB: Zone path

QB: Pre-snap reads the grass concept side and then the now screen side and executes a throw if they are gifts. If the alignment of the defense prevents a pre-snap throw, meshes with the back and reads the C gap defender; if he squeezes, executes the grass concept (post-snap) or runs the ball accordingly.

PLAY #36: INSIDE ZONE (SNIFFER)/NOW 2

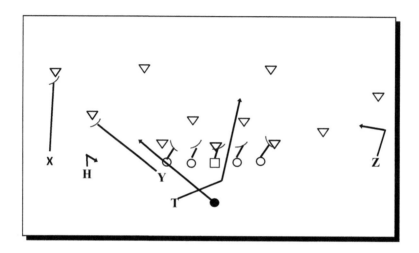

Blocking Rules:

Z: Grass

X: Stalk blocks #1

H: Bubble

Y: Stalk blocks #2

RT: Zone

RG: Zone

C: Zone

LG: Zone

LT: Zone

TB: Zone path

QB: Pre-snap reads the grass concept side and then the now screen side and executes a throw if they are gifts. If the alignment of the defense prevents a pre-snap throw, meshes with the back and reads the C gap defender; if he squeezes, executes the now screen (post-snap) or runs the ball accordingly.

PLAY #37: INSIDE ZONE (SNIFFER)/TIDE

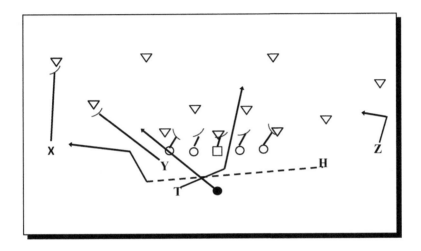

Blocking Rules:

Z: Grass

X: Stalk blocks #1

H: Fakes jet sweep; executes a down-the-line flat route

Y: Stalk blocks #2

RT: Zone

RG: Zone

C: Zone

LG: Zone

LT: Zone

TB: Zone path

QB: Pre-snap reads the grass concept side and executes a throw if there is a gift. If the alignment of the defense prevents a pre-snap throw, meshes with the back and reads the C gap defender; if he squeezes, executes the tide concept (post-snap) or runs the ball accordingly.

PLAY #38: INSIDE ZONE (SNIFFER)/TIDE-POP

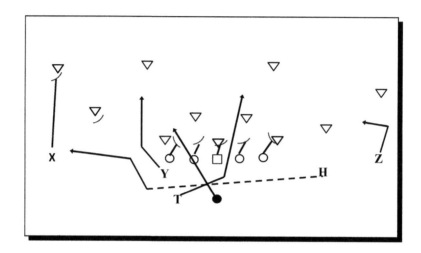

Blocking Rules:

Z: Grass

X: Stalk blocks #1

H: Fakes jet sweep; executes a down-the-line flat route

Y: Pop

RT: Zone

RG: Zone

C: Zone

LG: Zone

LT: Zone

TB: Zone path

QB: Pre-snap reads the grass concept side and executes a throw if there is a gift. If the alignment of the defense prevents a pre-snap throw, meshes with the back and reads the C gap defender; if he squeezes, executes the tide concept, pop pass (post-snap) or runs the ball accordingly.

PLAY #39: INSIDE ZONE (SNIFFER) 2X2/POP

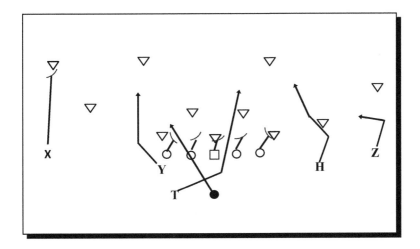

Blocking Rules:

Z: Grass

X: Stalk blocks #1

H: Grass

Y: Pop

RT: Zone

RG: Zone

C: Zone

LG: Zone

LT: Zone

TB: Zone path

QB: Pre-snap reads the grass concept side and executes a throw if there is a gift. If the alignment of the defense prevents a pre-snap throw, meshes with the back and reads the C gap defender; if he squeezes, executes the pop pass (post-snap) or runs the ball accordingly.

PLAY #40: INSIDE ZONE (SNIFFER) 3X1/POP

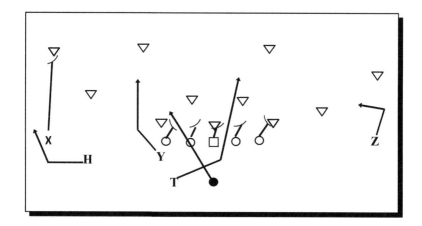

Blocking Rules:

Z: Grass

X: Stalk blocks #1

H: Bubble

Y: Pop

RT: Zone

RG: Zone

C: Zone

LG: Zone

LT: Zone

TB: Zone path

QB: Pre-snap reads the grass concept side and executes a throw if there is a gift. If the alignment of the defense prevents a pre-snap throw, meshes with the back and reads the C gap defender; if he squeezes, executes the pop pass (post-snap) or runs the ball accordingly.

PLAY #41: INSIDE ZONE (SNIFFER) 3X2/POP

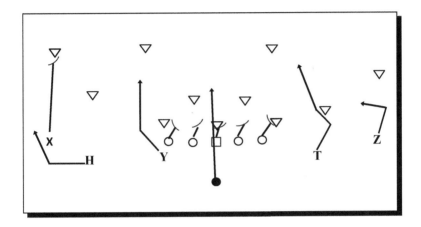

Blocking Rules:

Z: Grass

X: Stalk

H: Bubble

Y: Pop

RT: Zone

RG: Zone

C: Zone

LG: Zone

LT: Zone

TB: Grass

QB: Pre-snap reads the grass concept side and executes a throw if there is a gift. If the alignment of the defense prevents a pre-snap throw, meshes with the back and reads the C gap defender; if he squeezes, executes the pop pass (post-snap) or runs the ball accordingly.

PLAY #42: INSIDE ZONE (REO)/NOW 1

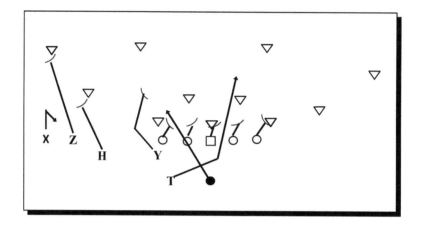

Blocking Rules:

Z: Stalk blocks #1

X: Screen

H: Stalk blocks #2

Y: Arc blocks the scrape player

RT: Zone

RG: Zone

C: Zone

LG: Zone

LT: Zone

TB: Zone path

QB: Pre-snap reads the now screen concept side and executes a throw if there is a gift. If the alignment of the defense prevents a pre-snap throw, meshes with the back and reads the C gap defender; if he squeezes, executes the now screen (post-snap) or runs the ball accordingly.

PLAY #43: INSIDE ZONE (REO)/NOW 3

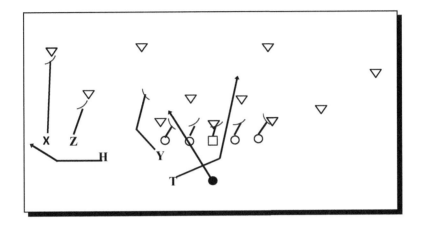

Blocking Rules:

Z: Stalk blocks #2

X: Stalk blocks #1

H: Screen

Y: Arc blocks the scrape player

RT: Zone

RG: Zone

C: Zone

LG: Zone

LT: Zone

TB: Zone path

QB: Pre-snap reads the now screen concept side and executes a throw if there is a gift. If the alignment of the defense prevents a pre-snap throw, meshes with the back and reads the C gap defender; if he squeezes, executes the now screen (post-snap) or runs the ball accordingly.

PLAY #44: POWER/NOW 1

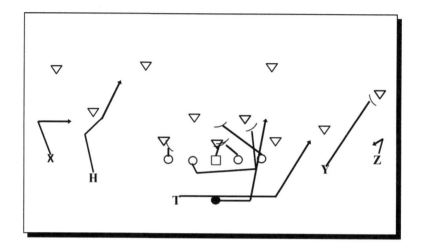

Blocking Rules:

Z: Screen

X: Grass

H: Grass

Y: Stalk blocks #1

RT: On to down

RG: On to down

C: On to down

LG: Pull

LT: Base

TB: Stretch path

QB: Pre-snap reads the grass concept side and the now screen side to determine whether or not to execute a throw if there is a gift. If the alignment of the defense prevents a pre-snap throw, meshes with the back and reads the C gap defender; if he squeezes, gives the ball to the back, and if he feathers, then runs the ball accordingly.

PLAY #45: POWER/ STICK CONCEPT

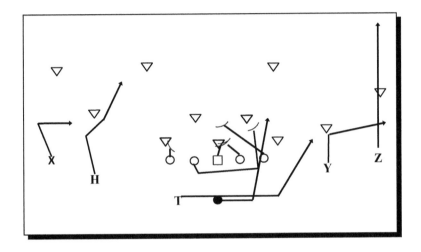

Blocking Rules:

Z: Fade

X: Grass

H: Grass

Y: Flat

RT: On to down

RG: On to down

C: On to down

LG: Pull

LT: Base

TB: Stretch path

QB: Pre-snap reads the grass concept side and the stick concept side to determine whether or not to execute a throw if there is a gift. If the alignment of the defense prevents a pre-snap throw, meshes with the back and reads the C gap defender; if he squeezes, gives the ball to the back, and if he feathers, then runs the ball accordingly.

PLAY #46: POWER (2X2 SNIFFER)/POP

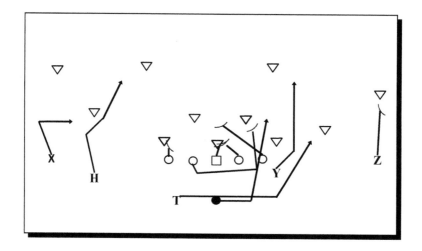

Blocking Rules:

Z: Stalk blocks #1

X: Grass

H: Grass

Y: Pop

RT: On to down

RG: On to down

C: On to down

LG: Pull

LT: Base

TB: Stretch path

QB: Pre-snap reads the grass concept side to determine whether or not to execute a throw if there is a gift. If the alignment of the defense prevents a pre-snap throw, meshes with the back and reads the C gap defender; if he squeezes, gives the ball to the back, and if he feathers, then runs the ball accordingly or throws the pop pass.

PLAY #47: POWER (3X1 SNIFFER)/POP

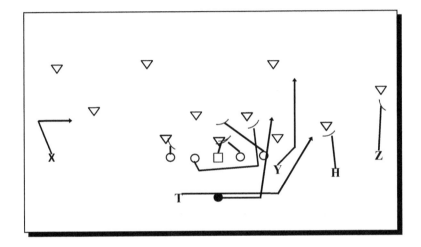

Blocking Rules:

Z: Stalk blocks #1

X: Grass

H: Stalk blocks #2

Y: Pop

RT: On to down

RG: On to down

C: On to down

LG: Pull

LT: Base

TB: Stretch path

QB: Pre-snap reads the grass concept side to determine whether or not to execute a throw if there is a gift. If the alignment of the defense prevents a pre-snap throw, meshes with the back and reads the C gap defender; if he squeezes, gives the ball to the back, and if he feathers, then runs the ball accordingly or throw the pop pass.

PLAY #48: POWER SHOVEL/NOW 1

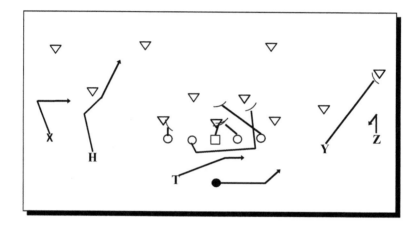

Blocking Rules:

Z: Screen

X: Grass

H: Grass

Y: Stalk blocks #1

RT: On to down

RG: On to down

C: On to down

LG: Pull

LT: Base

TB: Shovel path

QB: Pre-snap reads the grass concept side to determine whether or not to execute a throw if there is a gift. If the alignment of the defense prevents a pre-snap throw, open-steps and crosses over and reads the C gap defender; if he squeezes, pulls the ball and runs the ball accordingly or throws the pass. If the C gap defender feathers, shovels the ball to the back.

PLAY #49: POWER SHOVEL/NOW 2

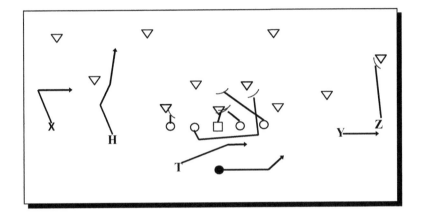

Blocking Rules:

Z: Stalk blocks #1

X: Grass

H: Grass

Y: Screen

RT: On to down

RG: On to down

C: On to down

LG: Pull

LT: Base

TB: Shovel path

QB: Pre-snap reads the grass concept side to determine whether or not to execute a throw if there is a gift. If the alignment of the defense prevents a pre-snap throw, open-steps and crosses over and reads the C gap defender; if he squeezes, pulls the ball and runs the ball accordingly or throws the pass. If the C gap defender feathers, shovels the ball to the back.

PLAY #50: POWER SHOVEL/NOW 3

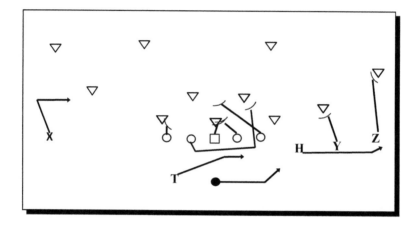

Blocking Rules:

Z: Stalk blocks #1

X: Grass

H: Screen

Y: Stalk blocks #2

RT: On to down

RG: On to down

C: On to down

LG: Pull

LT: Base

TB: Shovel path

QB: Pre-snap reads the grass concept side to determine whether or not to execute a throw if there is a gift. If the alignment of the defense prevents a pre-snap throw, open-steps and crosses over and reads the C gap defender; if he squeezes, pulls the ball and runs the ball accordingly or throws the pass. If the C gap defender feathers, shovels the ball to the back.

PLAY #51: POWER SHOVEL/ HITCH CONCEPT

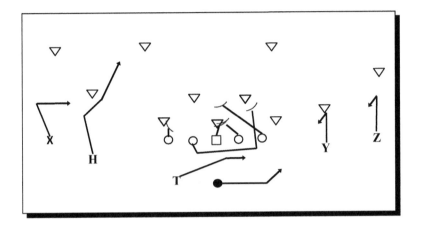

Blocking Rules:

Z: Hitch

X: Grass

H: Grass

Y: Hitch

RT: On to down

RG: On to down

C: On to down

LG: Pull

LT: Base

TB: Shovel path

QB: Pre-snap reads the grass concept side to determine whether or not to execute a throw if there is a gift. If the alignment of the defense prevents a pre-snap throw, open-steps and crosses over and reads the C gap defender; if he squeezes, pulls the ball and runs the ball accordingly or throws the pass. If the C gap defender feathers, shovels the ball to the back.

PLAY #52: POWER SHOVEL/ GRASS CONCEPT

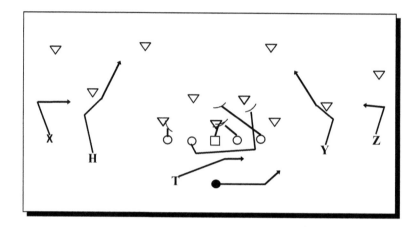

Blocking Rules:

Z: Grass

X: Grass

H: Grass

Y: Grass

RT: On to down

RG: On to down

C: On to down

LG: Pull

LT: Base

TB: Shovel path

QB: Pre-snap reads the grass concept side to determine whether or not to execute a throw if there is a gift. If the alignment of the defense prevents a pre-snap throw, open-steps and crosses over and reads the C gap defender; if he squeezes, pulls the ball and runs the ball accordingly or throws the pass. If the C gap defender feathers, shovels the ball to the back.

PLAY #53: POWER SHOVEL/ STOP CONCEPT

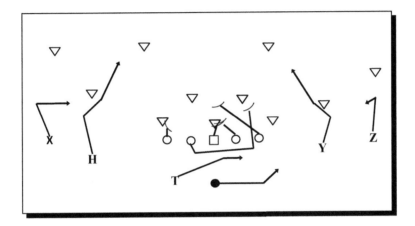

Blocking Rules:

Z: Stop

X: Grass

H: Grass

Y: Grass

RT: On to down

RG: On to down

C: On to down

LG: Pull

LT: Base

TB: Shovel path

QB: Pre-snap reads the grass concept side to determine whether or not to execute a throw if there is a gift. If the alignment of the defense prevents a pre-snap throw, open-steps and crosses over and reads the C gap defender; if he squeezes, pulls the ball and runs the ball accordingly or throws the pass. If the C gap defender feathers, shovels the ball to the back.

PLAY #54: POWER SHOVEL/ SNAG CONCEPT

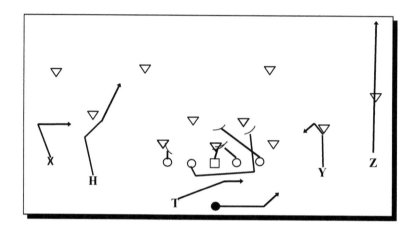

Blocking Rules:

Z: Fade

X: Grass

H: Grass

Y: Snag

RT: On to down

RG: On to down

C: On to down

LG: Pull

LT: Base

TB: Shovel path

QB: Pre-snap reads the grass concept side to determine whether or not to execute a throw if there is a gift. If the alignment of the defense prevents a pre-snap throw, open-steps and crosses over and reads the C gap defender; if he squeezes, pulls the ball and runs the ball accordingly or throws the pass. If the C gap defender feathers, shovels the ball to the back.

PLAY #55: POWER SHOVEL/ STICK CONCEPT

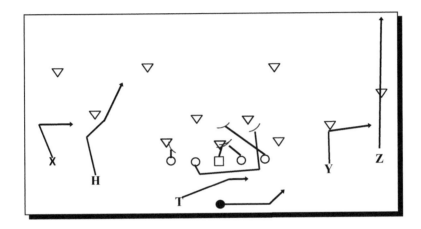

Blocking Rules:

Z: Fade

X: Grass

H: Grass

Y: Flat

RT: On to down

RG: On to down

C: On to down

LG: Pull

LT: Base

TB: Shovel path

QB: Pre-snap reads the grass concept side to determine whether or not to execute a throw if there is a gift. If the alignment of the defense prevents a pre-snap throw, open-steps and crosses over and reads the C gap defender; if he squeezes, pulls the ball and runs the ball accordingly or throws the pass. If the C gap defender feathers, shovels the ball to the back.

PLAY #56: POWER SHOVEL/ SPOT CONCEPT

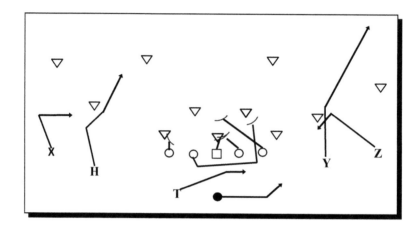

Blocking Rules:

Z: Spot

X: Grass

H: Grass

Y: Corner

RT: On to down

RG: On to down

C: On to down

LG: Pull

LT: Base

TB: Shovel path

QB: Pre-snap reads the grass concept side to determine whether or not to execute a throw if there is a gift. If the alignment of the defense prevents a pre-snap throw, open-steps and crosses over and reads the C gap defender; if he squeezes, pulls the ball and runs the ball accordingly or throws the pass. If the C gap defender feathers, shovels the ball to the back.

PLAY #57: COUNTER/NOW 1

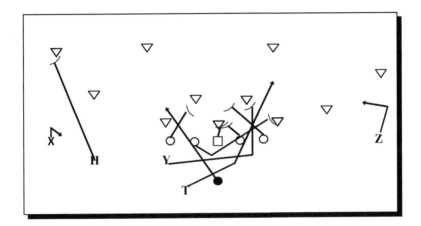

Blocking Rules:

Z: Grass

X: Screen

H: Stalk blocks #1

Y: Pull and lead

RT: On to down

RG: On to down

C: Blocks back

LG: Pull and trap

LT: Scoops B gap

TB: Zone path

QB: Pre-snap reads the grass concept side and executes a throw if there is a gift. If the alignment of the defense prevents a pre-snap throw, meshes with the back and reads the C gap defender; if he squeezes, executes the now screen (post-snap) or runs the ball accordingly.

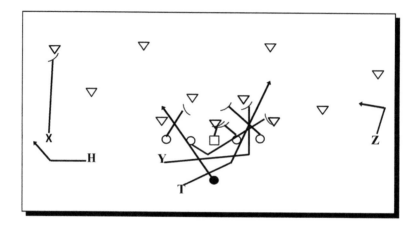

Blocking Rules:

Z: Grass

X: Stalk blocks #1

H: Screen

Y: Pull and lead

RT: On to down

RG: On to down

C: Blocks back

LG: Pull and trap

LT: Scoops B gap

TB: Zone path

QB: Pre-snap reads the grass concept side and executes a throw if there is a gift. If the alignment of the defense prevents a pre-snap throw, meshes with the back and reads the C gap defender; if he squeezes, executes the now screen (post-snap) or runs the ball accordingly.

PLAY #59: COUNTER/NOW 4

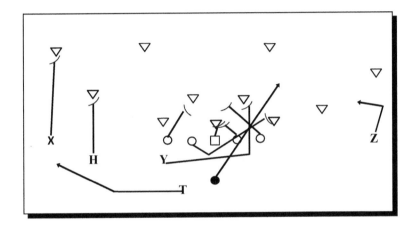

Blocking Rules:

Z: Grass

X: Stalk blocks #1

H: Stalk blocks #2

Y: Pull and lead

RT: On to down

RG: On to down

C: Blocks back

LG: Pull and trap

LT: Scoops B gap

TB: Swing screen

QB: Pre-snap reads the grass concept side and executes a throw if there is a gift. If the alignment of the defense prevents a pre-snap throw, reads the third defender from the sideline at the second level; if he squeezes, executes the swing screen (post-snap) or runs the ball accordingly.

PLAY #60: COUNTER/ HITCH CONCEPT

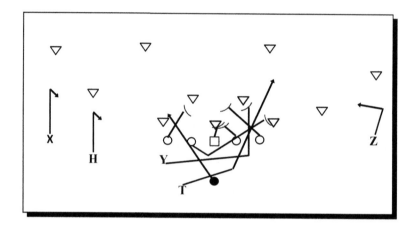

Blocking Rules:

Z: Grass

X: Hitch

H: Hitch

Y: Pull and lead

RT: On to down

RG: On to down

C- Blocks back

LG: Pull and trap

LT: Scoops B gap

TB: Zone path

QB: Pre-snap reads the grass concept side and executes a throw if there is a gift. If the alignment of the defense prevents a pre-snap throw, meshes with the back and reads the C gap defender; if he squeezes, executes the hitch concept (post-snap) or runs the ball accordingly.

PLAY #61: COUNTER/ GRASS CONCEPT

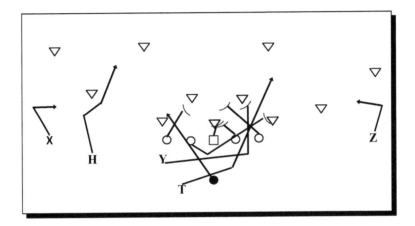

Blocking Rules:

Z: Grass

X: Grass

H: Grass

Y: Pull and lead

RT: On to down

RG: On to down

C: Blocks back

LG: Pull and trap

LT: Scoops B gap

TB: Zone path

QB: Pre-snap reads the grass concept side and executes a throw if there is a gift. If the alignment of the defense prevents a pre-snap throw, meshes with the back and reads the C gap defender; if he squeezes, executes the grass concept (post-snap) or runs the ball accordingly.

PLAY #62: COUNTER/ STOP CONCEPT

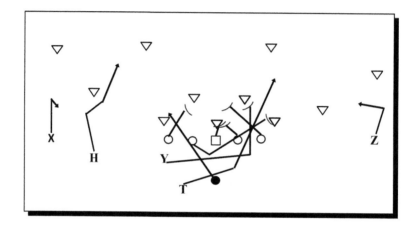

Blocking Rules:

Z: Grass

X: Stop

H: Grass

Y: Pull and lead

RT: On to down

RG: On to down

C: Blocks back

LG: Pull and trap

LT: Scoops B gap

TB: Zone path

QB: Pre-snap reads the grass concept side and executes a throw if there is a gift. If the alignment of the defense prevents a pre-snap throw, meshes with the back and reads the C gap defender; if he squeezes, executes the stop concept (post-snap) or runs the ball accordingly.

PLAY #63: COUNTER/ SNAG CONCEPT

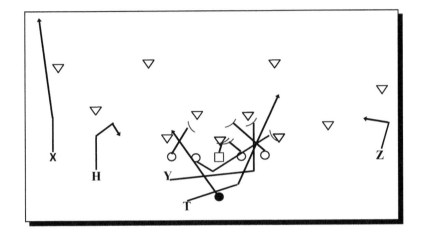

Blocking Rules:

Z: Grass

X: Fade

H: Snag

Y: Pull and lead

RT: On to down

RG: On to down

C: Blocks back

LG: Pull and trap

LT: Scoops B gap

TB: Zone path

QB: Pre-snap reads the grass concept side and executes a throw if there is a gift. If the alignment of the defense prevents a pre-snap throw, meshes with the back and reads the C gap defender; if he squeezes, executes the snag concept (post-snap) or runs the ball accordingly.

PLAY #64: COUNTER/ STICK CONCEPT

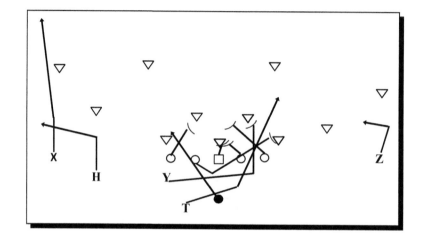

Blocking Rules:

Z: Grass

X: Fade

H: Flat

Y: Pull and lead

RT: On to down

RG: On to down

C: Blocks back

LG: Pull and trap

LT: Scoops B gap

TB: Zone path

QB: Pre-snap reads the grass concept side and executes a throw if there is a gift. If the alignment of the defense prevents a pre-snap throw, meshes with the back and reads the C gap defender; if he squeezes, executes the stick concept (post-snap) or runs the ball accordingly.

PLAY #65: COUNTER/ SPOT CONCEPT

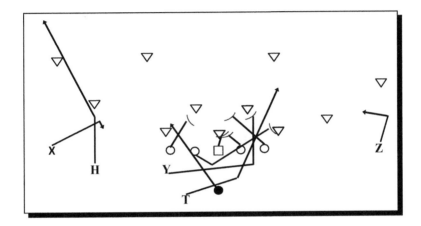

Blocking Rules:

Z: Grass

X: Spot

H: Corner

Y: Pull and lead

RT: On to down

RG: On to down

C: Blocks back

LG: Pull and trap

LT: Scoops B gap

TB: Zone path

QB: Pre-snap reads the grass concept side and executes a throw if there is a gift. If the alignment of the defense prevents a pre-snap throw, meshes with the back and reads the C gap defender; if he squeezes, executes the spot concept (post-snap) or runs the ball accordingly.

PLAY #66: COUNTER/ TAPER CONCEPT

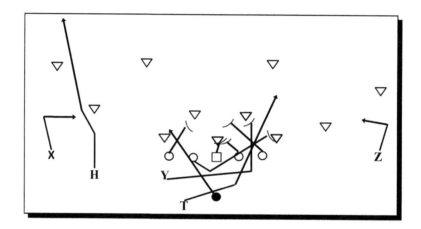

Blocking Rules:

Z: Grass

X: Speed in

H: Taper fade

Y: Pull and lead

RT: On to down

RG: On to down

C: Blocks back

LG: Pull and trap

LT: Scoops B gap

TB: Zone path

QB: Pre-snap reads the grass concept side and executes a throw if there is a gift. If the alignment of the defense prevents a pre-snap throw, meshes with the back and reads the C gap defender; if he squeezes, executes the taper concept (post-snap) or runs the ball accordingly.

PLAY #67: COUNTER/ SIT CONCEPT

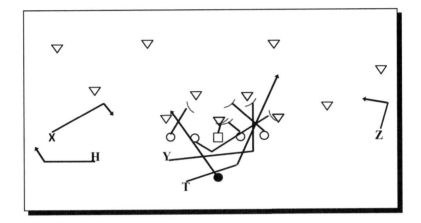

Blocking Rules:

Z: Grass

X: Sit

H: Bubble

Y: Pull and lead

RT: On to down

RG: On to down

C: Blocks back

LG: Pull and trap

LT: Scoops B gap

TB: Zone path

QB: Pre-snap reads the grass concept side and executes a throw if there is a gift. If the alignment of the defense prevents a pre-snap throw, meshes with the back and reads the C gap defender; if he squeezes, executes the sit concept (post-snap) or runs the ball accordingly.

PLAY #68: COUNTER/ SLANT OPTION CONCEPT

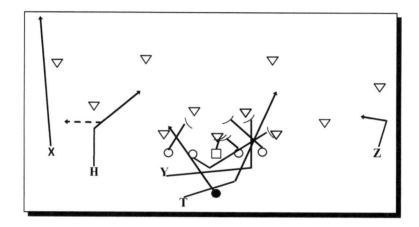

Blocking Rules:

Z: Grass

X: Fade

H: Slant option

Y: Pull and lead

RT: On to down

RG: On to down

C: Blocks back

LG: Pull and trap

LT: Scoops B gap

TB: Zone path

QB: Pre-snap reads the grass concept side and executes a throw if there is a gift. If the alignment of the defense prevents a pre-snap throw, meshes with the back and reads the C gap defender; if he squeezes, executes the slant option concept (post-snap) or runs the ball accordingly.

PLAY #69: COUNTER/ SLANT FLAT CONCEPT

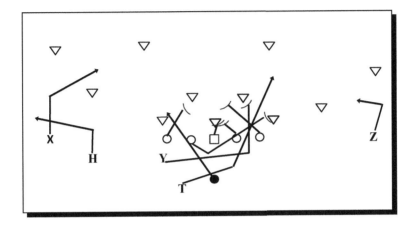

Blocking Rules:

Z: Grass

X: Slant

H: Flat

Y: Pull and lead

RT: On to down

RG: On to down

C: Blocks back

LG: Pull and trap

LT: Scoops B gap

TB: Zone path

QB: Pre-snap reads the grass concept side and executes a throw if there is a gift. If the alignment of the defense prevents a pre-snap throw, meshes with the back and reads the C gap defender; if he squeezes, executes the slant flat concept (post-snap) or runs the ball accordingly.

PLAY #70: COUNTER/ STUTTER CONCEPT

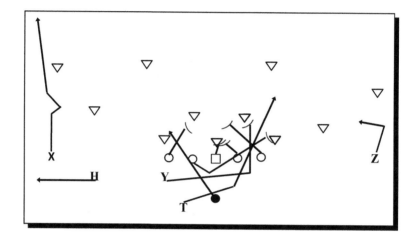

Blocking Rules:

Z: Grass

X: Stutter fade

H: Bubble

Y: Pull and lead

RT: On to down

RG: On to down

C: Blocks back

LG: Pull and trap

LT: Scoop B gap

TB: Zone path

QB: Pre-snap reads the grass concept side and executes a throw if there is a gift. If the alignment of the defense prevents a pre-snap throw, meshes with the back and reads the C gap defender; if he squeezes, executes the stutter concept (post-snap) or run the ball accordingly.

PLAY #71: COUNTER RELEASE/NOW 1

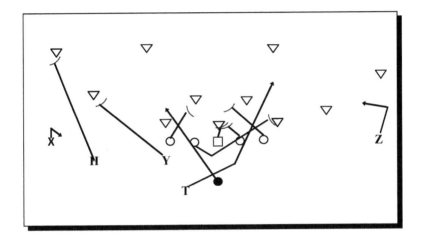

Blocking Rules:

Z: Grass

X: Screen

H: Stalk blocks #1

Y: Releases and stalk blocks #2

RT: On to down

RG: On to down

C: Blocks back

LG: Pull and trap

LT: Scoops B gap

TB: Zone path

QB: Pre-snap reads the grass concept side and executes a throw if there is a gift. If the alignment of the defense prevents a pre-snap throw, meshes with the back and reads the C gap defender; if he squeezes, executes the now screen (post-snap) or runs the ball accordingly.

PLAY #72: COUNTER RELEASE/NOW 2

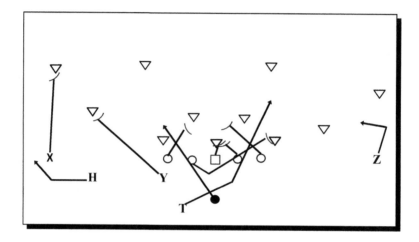

Blocking Rules:

Z: Grass

X: Stalk blocks #1

H: Screen

Y: Releases and stalk blocks #2

RT: On to down

RG: On to down

C: Blocks back

LG: Pull and trap

LT: Scoops B gap

TB: Zone path

QB: Pre-snap reads the grass concept side and executes a throw if there is a gift. If the alignment of the defense prevents a pre-snap throw, meshes with the back and reads the C gap defender; if he squeezes, executes the now screen (post-snap) or runs the ball accordingly.

PLAY #73: COUNTER RELEASE/NOW 3

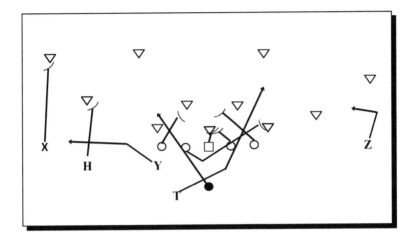

Blocking Rules:

Z: Grass

X: Stalk blocks #1

H: Stalk blocks #2

Y: Release and screen

RT: On to down

RG: On to down

C: Blocks back

LG: Pull and trap

LT: Scoops B gap

TB: Zone path

QB: Pre-snap reads the grass concept side and executes a throw if there is a gift. If the alignment of the defense prevents a pre-snap throw, meshes with the back and reads the C gap defender; if he squeezes, executes the now screen (post-snap) or runs the ball accordingly.

PLAY #74: COUNTER RELEASE/NOW 4

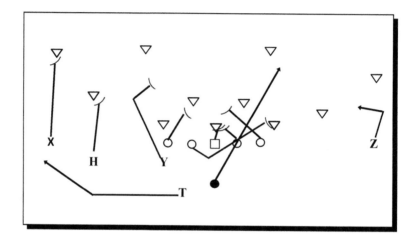

Blocking Rules:

Z: Grass

X: Stalk blocks #1

H: Stalk blocks #2

Y: Releases and stalk blocks #3

RT: On to down

RG: On to down

C: Blocks back

LG: Pull and trap

LT: Scoops B gap

TB: Swing screen

QB: Pre-snap reads the grass concept side and executes a throw if there is a gift. If the alignment of the defense prevents a pre-snap throw, reads the third defender from the sideline at the second level; if he squeezes, executes the swing screen (post-snap) or runs the ball accordingly.

PLAY #75: COUNTER RELEASE/HITCH CONCEPT

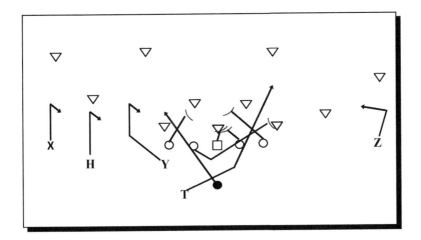

Blocking Rules:

Z: Grass

X: Hitch

H: Hitch

Y: Release and hitch

RT: On to down

RG: On to down

C: Blocks back

LG: Pull and trap

LT: Scoops B gap

TB: Zone path

QB: Pre-snap reads the grass concept side and executes a throw if there is a gift. If the alignment of the defense prevents a pre-snap throw, meshes with the back and reads the C gap defender; if he squeezes, executes the hitch concept (post-snap) or runs the ball accordingly.

PLAY #76: COUNTER RELEASE/GRASS CONCEPT

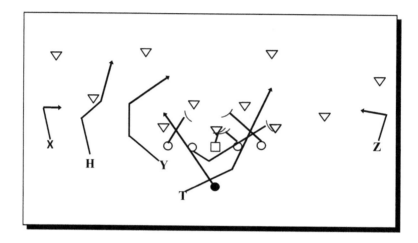

Blocking Rules:

Z: Grass

X: Grass

H: Grass

Y: Release and grass

RT: On to down

RG: On to down

C: Blocks back

LG: Pull and trap

LT: Scoops B gap

TB: Zone path

QB: Pre-snap reads the grass concept side and executes a throw if there is a gift. If the alignment of the defense prevents a pre-snap throw, meshes with the back and reads the C gap defender; if he squeezes, executes the grass concept (post-snap) or runs the ball accordingly.

PLAY #77: COUNTER RELEASE/STOP CONCEPT

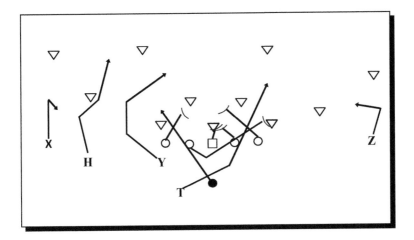

Blocking Rules:

Z: Grass

X: Stop

H: Grass

Y: Release and grass

RT: On to down

RG: On to down

C: Blocks back

LG: Pull and trap

LT: Scoops B gap

TB: Zone path

QB: Pre-snap reads the grass concept side and executes a throw if there is a gift. If the alignment of the defense prevents a pre-snap throw, meshes with the back and reads the C gap defender; if he squeezes, executes the stop concept (post-snap) or runs the ball accordingly.

PLAY #78: COUNTER RELEASE/SNAG CONCEPT

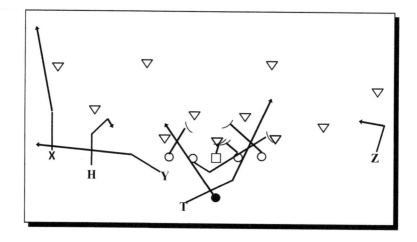

Blocking Rules:

Z: Grass

X: Fade

H: Snag

Y: Release and flat

RT: On to down

RG: On to down

C: Blocks back

LG: Pull and trap

LT: Scoops B gap

TB: Zone path

QB: Pre-snap reads the grass concept side and executes a throw if there is a gift. If the alignment of the defense prevents a pre-snap throw, meshes with the back and reads the C gap defender; if he squeezes, executes the snag concept (post-snap) or runs the ball accordingly.

PLAY #79: COUNTER RELEASE/STICK CONCEPT

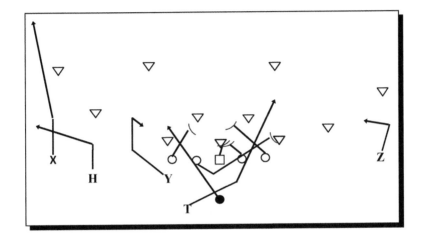

Blocking Rules:

Z: Grass

X: Fade

H: Flat

Y: Release and stick

RT: On to down

RG: On to down

C: Blocks back

LG: Pull and trap

LT: Scoops B gap

TB: Zone path

QB: Pre-snap reads the grass concept side and executes a throw if there is a gift. If the alignment of the defense prevents a pre-snap throw, meshes with the back and reads the C gap defender; if he squeezes, executes the stick concept (post-snap) or runs the ball accordingly.

PLAY #80: COUNTER RELEASE/SPOT CONCEPT

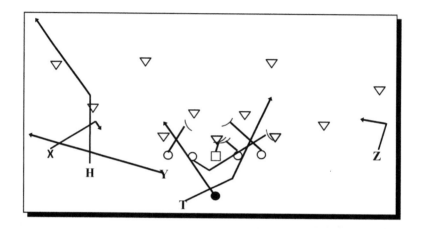

Blocking Rules:

Z: Grass

X: Spot

H: Corner

Y: Release and flat

RT: On to down

RG: On to down

C: Blocks back

LG: Pull and trap

LT: Scoops B gap

TB: Zone path

QB: Pre-snap reads the grass concept side and executes a throw if there is a gift. If the alignment of the defense prevents a pre-snap throw, meshes with the back and reads the C gap defender; if he squeezes, executes the spot concept (post-snap) or runs the ball accordingly.

PLAY #81: COUNTER RELEASE/TAPER CONCEPT

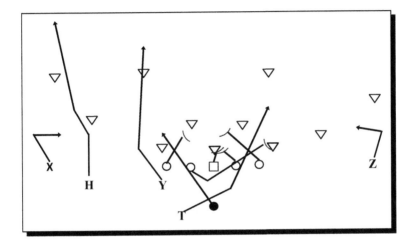

Blocking Rules:

Z: Grass

X: Speed in

H: Taper fade

Y: Release and seam

RT: On to down

RG: On to down

C: Blocks back

LG: Pull and trap

LT: Scoops B gap

TB: Zone path

QB: Pre-snap reads the grass concept side and executes a throw if there is a gift. If the alignment of the defense prevents a pre-snap throw, meshes with the back and reads the C gap defender; if he squeezes, executes the taper concept (post-snap) or runs the ball accordingly.

PLAY #82: COUNTER RELEASE/SIT CONCEPT

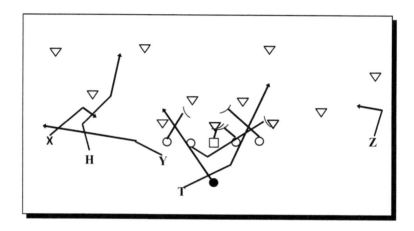

Blocking Rules:

Z: Grass

X: Sit

H: Broken arrow slant

Y: Release and flat

RT: On to down

RG: On to down

C: Blocks back

LG: Pull and trap

LT: Scoops B gap

TB: Zone path

QB: Pre-snap reads the grass concept side and executes a throw if there is a gift. If the alignment of the defense prevents a pre-snap throw, meshes with the back and reads the C gap defender; if he squeezes, executes the sit concept (post-snap) or runs the ball accordingly.

PLAY #83: COUNTER RELEASE/ SLANT OPTION CONCEPT

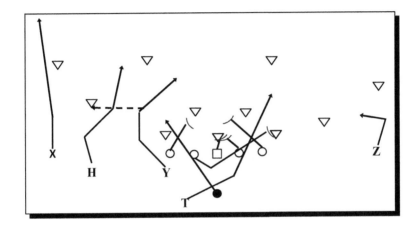

Blocking Rules:

Z: Grass

X: Fade

H: Broken arrow slant

Y: Release and slant option

RT: On to down

RG: On to down

C: Blocks back

LG: Pull and trap

LT: Scoops B gap

TB: Zone path

QB: Pre-snap reads the grass concept side and executes a throw if there is a gift. If the alignment of the defense prevents a pre-snap throw, meshes with the back and reads the C gap defender; if he squeezes, executes the slant option concept (post-snap) or runs the ball accordingly.

PLAY #84: COUNTER RELEASE/ SLANT FLAT CONCEPT

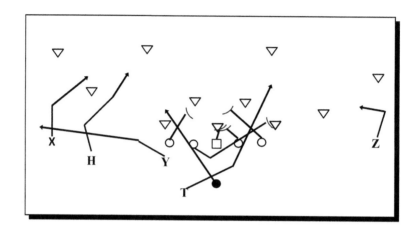

Blocking Rules:

Z: Grass

X: Slant

H: Broken arrow slant

Y: Release and flat

RT: On to down

RG: On to down

C: Blocks back

LG: Pull and trap

LT: Scoops B gap

TB: Zone path

QB: Pre-snap reads the grass concept side and executes a throw if there is a gift. If the alignment of the defense prevents a pre-snap throw, meshes with the back and reads the C gap defender; if he squeezes, executes the slant flat concept (post-snap) or runs the ball accordingly.

PLAY #85: COUNTER RELEASE/STUTTER CONCEPT

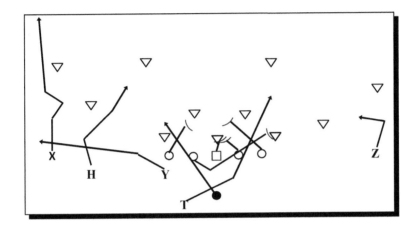

Blocking Rules:

Z: Grass

X: Stutter fade

H: Broken arrow slant

Y: Release and flat

RT: On to down

RG: On to down

C: Blocks back

LG: Pull and trap

LT: Scoops B gap

TB: Zone path

QB: Pre-snap reads the grass concept side and executes a throw if there is a gift. If the alignment of the defense prevents a pre-snap throw, meshes with the back and reads the C gap defender; if he squeezes, executes the stutter concept (post-snap) or runs the ball accordingly.

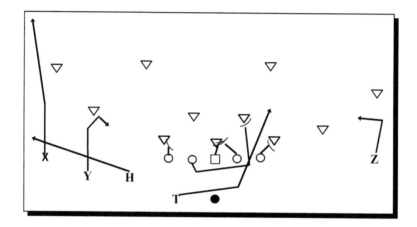

Blocking Rules:

Z: Grass

X: Fade

H: Flat

Y: Snag

RT: Turnout

RG: Man on

C: On to down

LG: Pulls for frontside linebacker

LT: Turnout

TB: Zone path

QB: Pre-snap reads the grass concept side and executes a throw if there is a gift. If the alignment of the defense prevents a pre-snap throw, meshes with the back and reads the third second-level defender from the sideline; if he squeezes, executes the snag concept (post-snap) or hands off the ball accordingly.

PLAY #87: ONE-BACK POWER/ SLANT OPTION CONCEPT

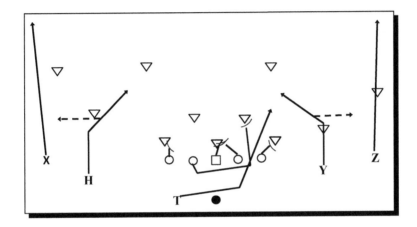

Blocking Rules:

Z: Fade

X: Fade

H: Slant option

Y: Slant option

RT: Turnout

RG: Man on

C: On to down

LG: Pulls for the frontside linebacker

LT: Turnout

TB: Zone path

QB: Pre-snap reads the slant option concept side toward the run side and executes a throw if there is a gift. If the alignment of the defense prevents a pre-snap throw, meshes with the back and reads the third second-level defender from the sideline; if he squeezes, executes the slant option concept (post-snap) or hands off the ball accordingly.

PLAY #88: INSERT INSIDE ZONE/STICK CONCEPT

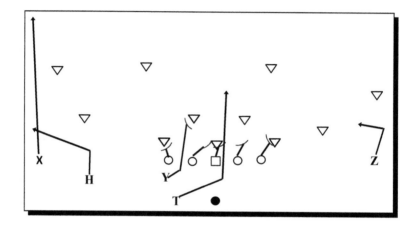

Blocking Rules:

Z: Grass

X: Fade

H: Flat

Y: Inserts into the first open gap backside of the zone call and blocks the linebacker

RT: Zone

RG: Zone

C: Zone

LG: Lock

LT: Lock

TB: Zone path

QB: Pre-snap reads the grass concept side and executes a throw if there is a gift. If the alignment of the defense prevents a pre-snap throw, meshes with the back and reads the second second-level defender from the sideline; if he squeezes, executes the stick concept (post-snap) or hands off the ball accordingly.

PLAY #89: SLOW INSIDE ZONE/SNAG CONCEPT

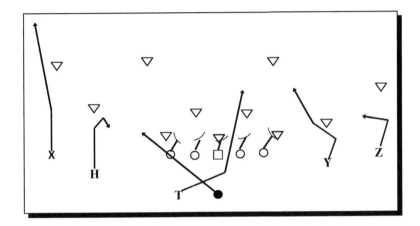

Blocking Rules:

Z: Grass

X: Fade

H: Snag

Y: Grass

RT: Slow zone, and remains on the block for an extra count

RG: Slow zone, and remains on the block for an extra count

C: Slow zone, and remains on the block for an extra count

LG: Slow zone, and remains on the block for an extra count

LT: Slow zone, and remains on the block for an extra count

TB: Zone path; lines up one step wider than normal

QB: Pre-snap reads the grass concept side and executes a throw if there is a gift. If the alignment of the defense prevents a pre-snap throw, meshes with the back and reads the C gap defender; if he squeezes, executes the snag concept (post-snap) or runs the ball accordingly.

PLAY #90: DOUBLE FOLD/NOW 3

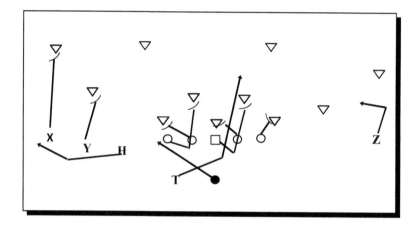

Blocking Rules:

Z: Grass

X: Stalk blocks #1

H: Screen

Y: Stalk blocks #2

RT: Zone/turnout

RG: Down

C: Fold

LG: Down

LT: Fold

TB: Zone path

QB: Pre-snap reads the grass concept side and executes a throw if there is a gift. If the alignment of the defense prevents a pre-snap throw, meshes with the back and reads the C gap defender; if he squeezes, executes the now screen (post-snap) or runs the ball accordingly.

PLAY #91: INSIDE ZONE X/NOW 2

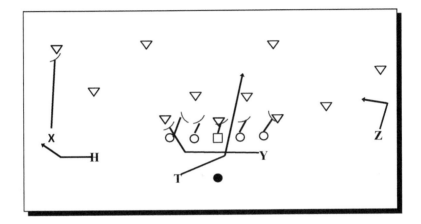

Blocking Rules:

Z: Grass

X: Stalk blocks #1

H: Screen

Y: Kick-out blocks the read key

RT: Zone

RG: Zone

C: Zone

LG: Zone

LT: Zone

TB: Zone path

QB: Pre-snap reads the grass concept side and executes a throw if there is a gift. If the alignment of the defense prevents a pre-snap throw, meshes with the back and reads the second second-level defender from the sideline; if he squeezes, executes the now screen (post-snap) or hands the ball off accordingly.

PLAY #92: INSIDE ZONE LADDER/NOW 2

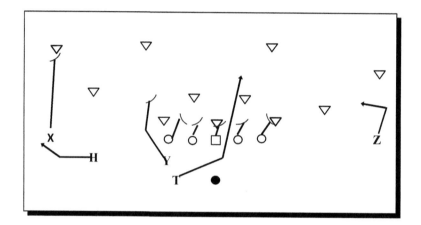

Blocking Rules:

Z: Grass

X: Stalk blocks #1

H: Bubble

Y: Load blocks the scrape player

RT: Zone

RG: Zone

C: Zone

LG: Zone

LT: Zone

TB: Zone path

QB: Pre-snap reads the grass concept side and executes a throw if there is a gift. If the alignment of the defense prevents a pre-snap throw, meshes with the back and reads the C gap defender; if he squeezes, executes the now screen (post-snap) or runs the ball accordingly.

PLAY #93: INSIDE ZONE LOCK/NOW 2

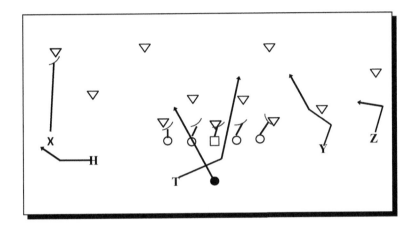

Blocking Rules:

Z: Grass

X: Stalk blocks #1

H: Bubble

Y: Grass

RT: Zone

RG: Zone

C: Zone

LG: Zone

LT: Zone

TB: Zone path

QB: Pre-snap reads the grass concept side and executes a throw if there is a gift. If the alignment of the defense prevents a pre-snap to the grass concept side, then also reads the now screen side as a pre-snap look. If both pre-snap looks are covered, then hands the ball off accordingly.

PLAY #94: INSIDE ZONE LOCK/FOUR VERTICALS

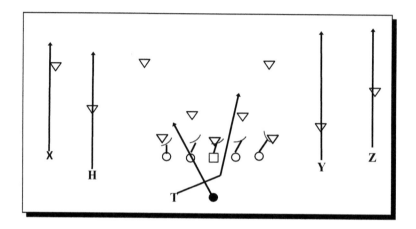

Blocking Rules:

Z: Fade

X: Fade

H: Quick seam

Y: Quick seam

RT: Zone

RG: Zone

C- Zone

LG: Zone

LT: Zone

TB: Zone path

QB: Pre-snap reads the four vertical concept and executes a throw if there is a gift. If the alignment of the defense prevents a pre-snap throw, meshes with the back and reads the movement of the second defenders from the sideline; if they squeeze, executes the pass play (post-snap) or hands off the ball accordingly.

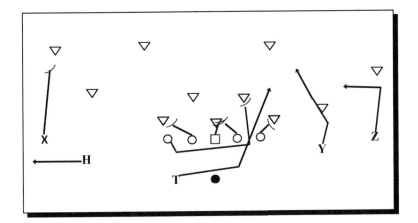

Blocking Rules:

Z: Grass

X: Stalk blocks #1

H: Screen

Y: Grass

RT: Zone

RG: Zone

C: Zone

LG: Zone

LT: Zone

TB: Zone path

QB: Pre-snap reads the grass concept side and executes a throw if there is a gift. If the alignment of the defense prevents a pre-snap throw, meshes with the back and reads the C gap defender; if he squeezes, executes the now screen (post-snap) or runs the ball accordingly.

PLAY #96: MIDLINE/ GRASS CONCEPT

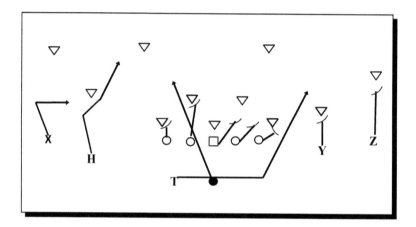

Blocking Rules:

Z: Stalk blocks #1

X: Grass

H: Grass

Y: Stalk blocks #2

RT: Stretch zone

RG: Stretch zone

C: Stretch zone

LG: Blocks the first linebacker backside

LT: Turnout

TB: Stretch zone path

QB: Pre-snap reads the grass concept side and executes a throw if there is a gift. If the alignment of the defense prevents a pre-snap throw, meshes with the back and reads the second down lineman backside from outside to inside; if he squeezes, executes the quarterback pull on the midline (post-snap) or hands the ball off accordingly.

PLAY #97: TOKYO (SLOW INSIDE ZONE)

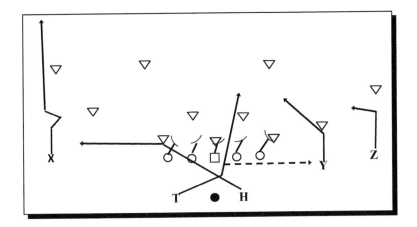

Blocking Rules:

Z: Stalk slant

X: Stutter fade

H: Chips the C gap player backside and runs a flat

Y: Stalk slant

RT: Slow zone

RG: Slow zone

C: Slow zone

LG: Slow zone

LT: Slow zone

TB: Zone path; if not given the ball, runs a flat

QB: Pre-snap reads the stalk slant concept side and executes a throw if there is a gift. If the alignment of the defense prevents a pre-snap throw, meshes with the back and reads the C gap defender; if he squeezes, executes the stutter fade concept (post-snap) or runs the ball accordingly.

PLAY #98: NINJA

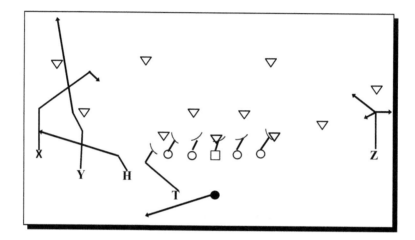

Blocking Rules:

Z: Hitch, slant, or out

X: Post curl

H: Flat

Y: Taper fade

RT: Slide right

RG: Slide right

C: Slide right

LG: Slide right

LT: Slide right

TB: Sets wide and pins the C gap defender

QB: Pre-snap reads the single-receiver side and executes a throw if there is a gift. If the alignment of the defense prevents a pre-snap throw, pump fakes and rolls around the pinned C gap defender; if he squeezes, executes the three-receiver side concept (post-snap) or runs the ball accordingly.

PLAY #99: TRUCK/ GRASS CONCEPT

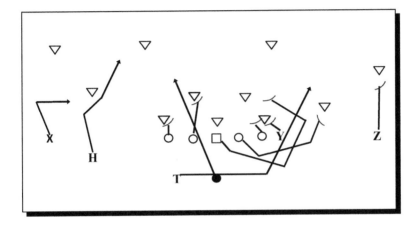

Blocking Rules:

Z: Stalk blocks #1

X: Grass

H: Grass

Y: On to down

RT: On to down

RG: Pull

C: Pull

LG: Blocks the first linebacker backside

LT: Turnout

TB: Stretch path

QB: Pre-snap reads the grass concept side and executes a throw if there is a gift. If the alignment of the defense prevents a pre-snap throw, meshes with the back and reads the second down lineman backside from outside to inside; if he squeezes, executes the quarterback midline (post-snap) accordingly.

PLAY #100: OUTSIDE ZONE (BULLDOG)/GRASS CONCEPT

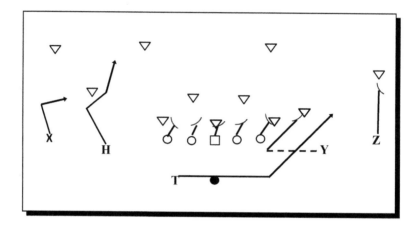

Blocking Rules:

Z: Stalk blocks #1

X: Grass

H: Grass

Y: Motions to a snigger alignment and blocks the stretch zone

RT: Stretch zone

RG: Stretch zone

C: Stretch zone

LG: Stretch zone

LT: Stretch zone

TB: Stretch path

QB: Pre-snap reads the grass concept side and executes a throw if there is a gift. If the alignment of the defense prevents a pre-snap throw, meshes with the back and reads the C gap defender; if he squeezes, executes the grass concept (post-snap) or runs the ball accordingly.

PLAY #101: ONE-BACK POWER/ DOUBLE OPTION CONCEPT

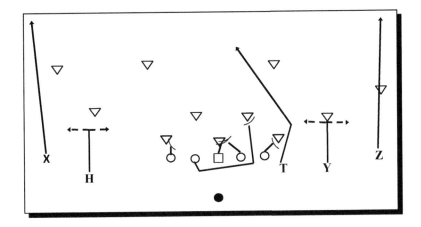

Blocking Rules:

Z: Fade

X: Fade

H: 5-yard option

Y: 5-yard option

RT: Turnout

RG: Man on

C: On to down

LG: Pulls for the frontside linebacker

LT: Turnout

TB: Seam gut

QB: Pre-snap reads the fade, seam, and option routes and executes a throw if there is a gift. If the alignment of the defense prevents a pre-snap throw, starts running the one-back power play; if the playside linebacker squeezes, executes the seam gut route (post-snap) or runs the ball accordingly.

CONCLUSION

The average coach faces many challenges today. Winning high school football games is a very difficult endeavor that requires the players, coaches, trainers, administration, fans, officials, the community, and the school at large to operate in cohesion and unity. The system that a coach chooses to employ is but a small part of the required apparatus necessary to win games. The air raid helps to recruit great players into your program, get fans excited about the style of play, attack defense from multiple points, and win games against vastly superior competition. The system has long allowed a coach to level the playing field to make to make their athletes more able to compete against superior talent. A wide variety of systems to employ are available these days, but three items seem to have always leveled the prospective playing field. The three main levelers of talent seem to have always been throwing the football, executing option football, and operating from a fast-paced tempo.

The consistent pattern in recent years has been for teams to move at break-neck pace into the world of the spread offense simply because it is in the news and carries a certain level of respect from pundits. The offense has certainly changed the game in ways that are very positive and will entertain fans and promote the sport past its more localized roots as a three-yards-and-cloud-of-dust game. Coaches of varied ages and backgrounds are now living in what amounts to a renaissance for offensive football. The game is evolving at such an accelerated pace that it is quite simply staggering how much information is available and digestible from a myriad of sources. However, it is necessary during this cultural and technological transformation that coaches analyze their systems and find the best way to teach. The game has really not changed as much as one might think. RPOs are really just triple option football that is run from high tempo and features at least as much passing as it does running of the football. The trifecta of passing, option, and tempo has found their melding point in the world of RPOs. This new version of the game is allowing coaches to utilize the same tactics that wishbone, wing-T, and shotgun spread coaches before them utilized. These new RPO coaches are armed with a unique system that levels the talent playing field and allows teams to compete against much bigger and stronger opponents. In a real-world sense, the RPO is almost to football what the three-point shot was to basketball: a change in the game that has caused defenses to completely reinvent themselves and forces offensive coaches to constantly study and utilize their new-found advantage.

While this work has not provided every idea as in pertains to the RPO style of football, it has attempted to provide the reader a glimpse into what is possible with RPOs. The style of football is constantly evolving and is doing so at an accelerated pace in comparison to years past. The concepts discussed in this book are the tip of the iceberg into what is actually possible with the system. As defenses attempt to play more pattern reading and man coverage styles to combat RPOs, the offense evolution will continue to drive the game to new and varying degrees of excitement. This work hopefully takes its place as the first definitive account of RPO playbooks that will certainly grow in complexity and number in the years to come.

ABOUT THE AUTHOR

Rich Hargitt has been a football coach since 1999. He has served as a head football coach and offensive coordinator at the high school level in Illinois, Indiana, North Carolina, and South Carolina. In 2010, he earned a master's of arts degree in physical education with coaching specialization from Ball State University.

Hargitt's teams have utilized the air raid offense to upset several quality teams, and the offense has produced school record-holders in rushing and passing. Coach Hargitt's first air raid quarterback, Mitch Niekamp, holds several college records at Illinois College and is currently a starting quarterback in Europe's professional leagues.

Hargitt previously contributed to a six-part video series on the spread wing-T offense for *American Football Monthly* and has been published numerous times in coaching journals on the air raid offense. He has spoken for both the Nike Coach of the Year Clinics and the Glazier Clinics about the air raid offense.

Hargitt's first book, *101 Shotgun Wing-T Plays*, was published by Coaches Choice in 2012. His second book, *101 Air Raid Plays*, was published by Coaches Choice in 2013. Hargitt's third book, *Coaching the Air Raid Offense*, was published in 2014. Hargitt's fourth and fifth books, *Packaging Plays in the Air Raid Offense* and *Play Calling for the Air Raid Offense*, were published in January of 2015. Coach Hargitt has also collaborated with Coaches Choice on a series of DVDs detailing the air raid offense.

In 2011, Hargitt brought the air raid offense to Nation Ford High School, where he helped lead the Falcons to their first non-losing season, first AAA Region victory, first AAA playoff berth, and first AAA playoff victory. In 2012, Hargitt's offense broke the school single-game and single-season offensive records for passing yards, touchdowns, and points scored. Also in 2012, Hargitt helped lead Nation Ford High School to the AAAA playoffs for the first time in school history. In 2013, Hargitt helped lead the Ashbrook Greenwave to the second round of NCHSAA AAA playoffs and a 9-4 overall record.

Hargitt is currently the assistant head coach and offensive coordinator at Southside High School in Greenville, South Carolina. Previously, he served as the assistant head coach/offensive coordinator at Eastside High School in Taylors, South Carolina. In 2015, Hargitt's offense achieved a statewide Top 10 ranking, averaged 383 yards per game (231 passing, 152 rushing), finished ranked in the Top 10 of the state and Top 5 of

AAA in passing, achieved second non-losing season in 13 years. In 2016, the offense improved even further as the team advanced to the SCHSL AAAA playoffs. In addition, the offense averaged 488 yards per game (286 passing, 202 rushing) and 41 points per game in the regular season and finished the season in AAAA ranked fourth in rushing (2,127 yards), third in rushing touchdowns (27), first in passing (3,311 yards), first in yards passing per game (301), first in pass completions (257), first in pass attempts (365), first in passing touchdowns (37), first in completion percentage (70 percent), first in touchdowns scored (65), first in scoring (453), first in PATs made (53), and first in total yardage from scrimmage (5,438 yards). The offense also led the state of South Carolina in total yardage from scrimmage (5,438 yards). The 2016 offense also featured a quarterback that completed the third most passes in a game and third most touchdown passes in a single game in state history. In addition, the offense featured a receiver that the fourth most passes in a single game and sixth most passes in a season in state history.

Since 2011, Hargitt's teams have amassed 24,816 total yards with 14,698 of those yards coming through the air and 10,118 yards on the ground. Hargitt resides in Taylors, South Carolina with his wife Lisa and their sons Griffin and Graham.